Air Force

Heather DiLorenzo Williams
and Warren Rylands

EYEDISCOVER

Go to www.eyediscover.com and enter this book's unique code.

BOOK CODE

AVW63382

EYEDISCOVER brings you optic readalongs that support active learning.

Published by AV² by Weigl
350 5th Avenue, 59th Floor New York, NY 10118
Website: www.eyediscover.com

Library of Congress Control Number: 2018953521

ISBN 978-1-4896-8025-9 (hardcover)

Printed in Brainerd, Minnesota,United States
1 2 3 4 5 6 7 8 9 0 22 21 20 19 18

082018
120917

Project Coordinators: John Willis
Designer: Mandy Christiansen

Weigl acknowledges Getty Images, Alamy, Shutterstock, and the U.S. Air Force as the primary image suppliers for this title.

EYEDISCOVER provides enriched content, optimized for tablet use, that supplements and complements this book. EYEDISCOVER books strive to create inspired learning and engage young minds in a total learning experience.

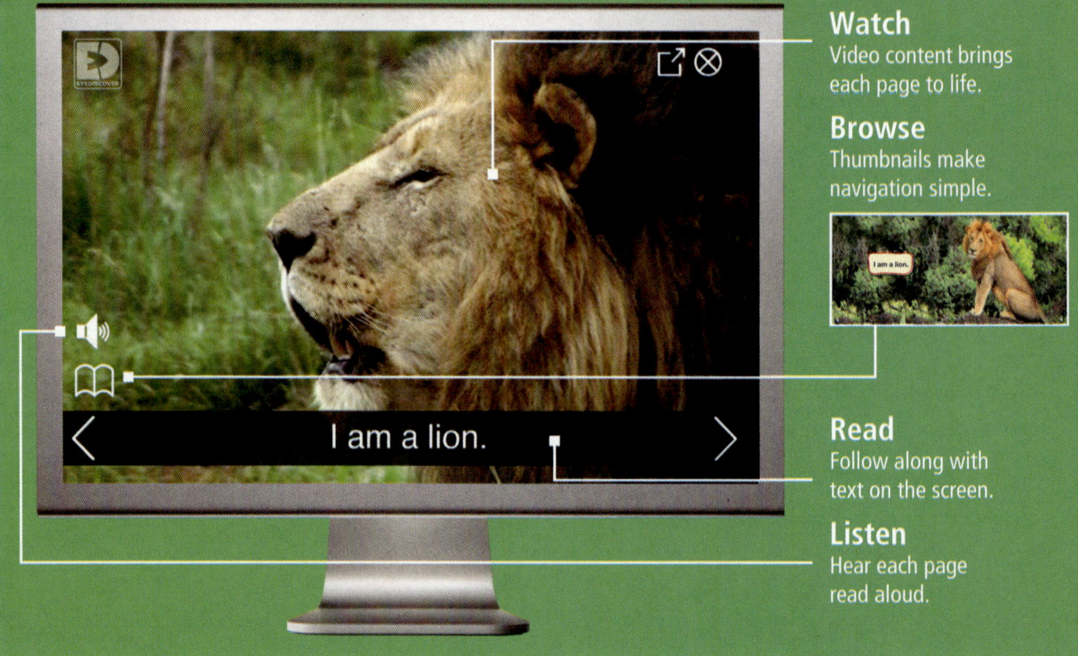

Watch
Video content brings each page to life.

Browse
Thumbnails make navigation simple.

Read
Follow along with text on the screen.

Listen
Hear each page read aloud.

Your EYEDISCOVER Optic Readalongs come alive with...

Audio
Listen to the entire book read aloud.

Video
High resolution videos turn each spread into an optic readalong.

OPTIMIZED FOR

- ✓ TABLETS
- ✓ WHITEBOARDS
- ✓ COMPUTERS
- ✓ AND MUCH MORE!

Air Force

In this book, you will learn about

- how it started
- what it does
- the tools it has

and much more!

The U.S. Air Force is one of the five branches of the United States Armed Forces.

6

The Air Force uses planes and helicopters to protect Americans during war.

The Air Force was founded in 1947. Before that, it was part of the U.S. Army.

9

Officers are trained at the Air Force Academy in Colorado Springs, Colorado.

WARNING - DO NOT CUT CANOPY
WITHIN 3 INCHES OF CANOPY FRAM
DANGER
EJECTION SEAT

A person needs to be between 18 and 28 years old to apply to be a pilot in the Air Force. They also need a college degree and one year of pilot school.

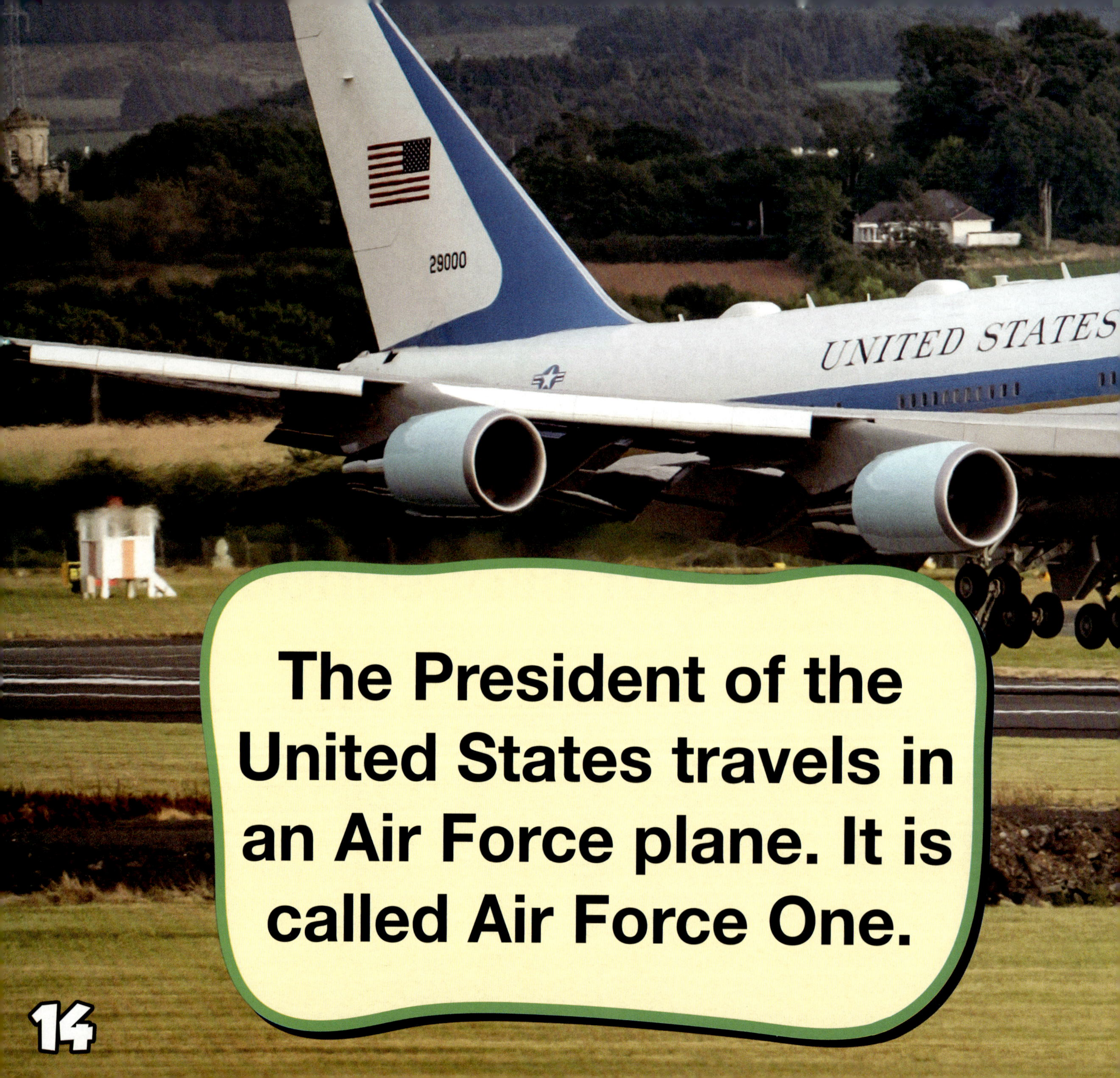

The President of the United States travels in an Air Force plane. It is called Air Force One.

F AMERICA

The F-16 is the most popular fighter plane in the world. There are more than 1,000 being used in the Air Force today.

305

A stealth bomber uses special technology to help it avoid being seen by enemy radar.

The three core values of the U.S. Air Force are Integrity First, Service Before Self, and Excellence in All We Do.

KEITH
U.S. AIR FORCE

AIR FORCE BY THE NUMBERS

More than **300,000** Americans serve in the **Air Force** full-time.

An **F-16** can travel **1,500 miles per hour.** (2,414 kilometers per hour)

Two U.S. presidents served in the **Air Force.**

A person must be
17 years old
to enlist in the
Air Force.

A **Stealth Bomber** costs
$2 billion.

There are more than
200
career options
in the Air Force.

KEY WORDS

Research has shown that as much as 65 percent of all written material published in English is made up of 300 words. These 300 words cannot be taught using pictures or learned by sounding them out. They must be recognized by sight. This book contains 38 common sight words to help young readers improve their reading fluency and comprehension. This book also teaches young readers several important content words, such as proper nouns. These words are paired with pictures to aid in learning and improve understanding.

Page	Sight Words First Appearance
4	air, is, of, one, the
7	and, to
8	before, in, it, part, that, was
11	are, at
13	a, also, be, between, need, old, school, they, years
15	an
16	being, more, most, than, there, world
19	by, help
20	all, do, first, three, we

Page	Content Words First Appearance
4	Armed Forces, branches, United States, U.S. Air Force
7	Americans, helicopters, planes, war
8	Army
11	Air Force Academy, Colorado Springs, officers
13	college, degree, pilot
15	president
16	F-16
19	bomber, enemy, radar, stealth, technology
20	values

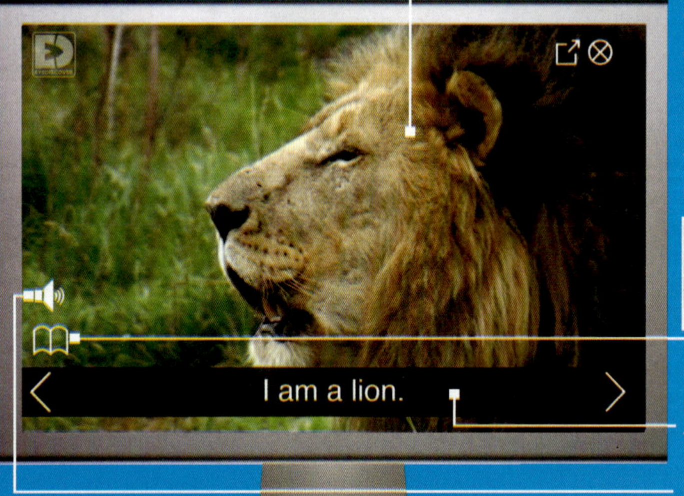

Watch
Video content brings each page to life.

Browse
Thumbnails make navigation simple.

Read
Follow along with text on the screen.

Listen
Hear each page read aloud.

Go to www.eyediscover.com and enter this book's unique code.

BOOK CODE

AVW63382